Handmade
Decorative Books

*Dedicated to my family and friends
for their support and encouragement.*

Handmade
Decorative Books

Sue Roddis

SEARCH PRESS

First published in Great Britain 2009

Search Press Limited
Wellwood, North Farm Road,
Tunbridge Wells, Kent TN2 3DR

Reprinted 2010

Text copyright © Sue Roddis 2009

Photographs by Debbie Patterson at Search Press Studios

Photographs and design copyright ©
Search Press Ltd 2009

ISBN: 978 1 84448 314 3

The Publishers and author can accept no responsibility for any consequences arising from the information, advice or instructions given in this publication.

Readers are permitted to reproduce any of the items in this book for their personal use, or for the purposes of selling for charity, free of charge and without the prior permission of the Publishers. Any use of the items for commercial purposes is not permitted without the prior permission of the Publishers.

Suppliers
If you have difficulty in obtaining any of the materials and equipment mentioned in this book, then please visit the Search Press website for details of suppliers:
www.searchpress.com

You are invited to visit the author's website at:
www.sroddis.blogspot.com

Publisher's note

All the step-by-step photographs in this book feature the author, Sue Roddis, demonstrating the craft of making handmade books. No models have been used.

Printed in Malaysia

Acknowledgements

There are a surprising number of people involved in the making of a book and I want to thank them all for their support and encouragement. Of course it goes almost without saying that there are my family and friends, but there is also Leandra from PaperArtsy who gave me the initial introduction to Roz from Search Press; Roz herself, who thought my book idea was good enough to go ahead with, and everyone else at Search Press: in particular my editor Edd, designer Juan and my photographer Deb for making the book look great!

I would also like to thank all the stamp companies whose images I have used throughout the book – keep up the good work producing fabulous images – the scrapbook paper companies for lovely papers to work with and Ranger Industries for producing my favourite ink pads in my favourite colours!

Last but not least I would like to thank my friend Wendy, of The Stamp Attic, who proclaims herself my biggest fan! I could not have done it without your support and faith in me!

Page 1: Home Sweet Home
This bright and cheerful star book shows that a little imagination goes a long way – handmade books provide a great outlet for your creativity!

Page 3: Autumn Leaves
This is the front cover of the project detailed on pages 64–75. The panels on the front mirror the pages inside, and the metal leaves gives a beautiful autumnal feel to the finished book.

Opposite: Birds on a Wire
A very unusual book; this is designed to be hung from a hook, but it looks just as attractive closed, thanks to the long tassel at the bottom.

Contents

Introduction

When I was a child, my mum made most of my clothes. She also made bridesmaids' dresses, toys and draught excluders. She was also an accomplished knitter, so I grew up surrounded by handmade things.

It is no surprise, then, that I turned to making things to fill my time when I took a break from work. Already a cross-stitcher, I enrolled on a City & Guilds course in creative embroidery, and at I discovered rubber stamping and card making about the same time. Although I thoroughly enjoyed embroidery, I soon realised that my heart lay with paper crafting.

I started with card making but soon wanted to move on to something more challenging. That turned out to be book making. Having had no formal training in the art of book making, I treat it very much as an extension of card making: for me, a book can be anything from a simple folded pamphlet to a more complicated star book. I find the idea of starting with a few tools, papers and embellishments and ending up with a book very satisfying. I hope I can pass on the fact that it can be as simple or as complicated as you want to make it.

The projects in this book start with simple and straightforward book ring and accordion-folded books and move on to flag, piano-hinge, star and other types of books. While the methods used to make the books can stay the same the colours and images used can be changed to suit your taste or the occasion.

So, using supplies that most paper crafters will already have on hand, let's get started making books!

Sue Roddis

Materials & equipment

Board, card and paper

The basic materials needed for book making are boards to use as covers, decorative papers to cover the boards and paper or card as pages. The type of book you are making will determine what you can use for the covers.

Ordinary card that you would use for card making can easily be used for smaller, lighter-weight books.

Book board can be covered with decorative papers of one sort or another and used for bigger books. Book board comes in different thicknesses so you can choose which is best suited to your project.

Mount board is sold to frame pictures, and it also makes good book covers.

Board is also useful for making binding guides: these are strips of card with holes punched through, which are used to mark the positions of the holes to be punched and used for the bindings. They can be saved and used several times for the same size and style of book.

Corrugated card can be used to cover boards or to make the actual cover itself if it is heavy enough.

Paper can be used both for pages and decoration. Good quality heavyweight paper makes for a high quality finished piece. Light weight paper is useful for covering boards, or making more delicate pages.

Handmade papers are great to use to cover boards. Care needs to be taken if they are very thin as the board can show through once the paper is wetted by the glue. If you want to use a very thin paper you might want to consider covering the boards with a plain paper first. Other handmade papers can be used directly to cover the boards.

Wrapping papers also offer a wide range of designs that can be used to cover your books.

Wallpapers are good for covering books, especially blown vinyl.

Brown paper also offers possibilities for book covering, and as pages. It can be stamped on to and have decorative ink and paint techniques applied to it before it is used to cover your books.

Scrapbook papers and **card** give an almost endless supply of patterns, colours and themes to suit any occasion.

The grain

Paper, card and board all have a grain. When paper and card are made, the fibres that make them up are pulled more in one direction than the other. This causes them to line up, giving more strength in one direction than the other.

To determine the direction of the grain in a piece of card or paper, fold it in half. There will be more resistance in one direction than the other. The direction which is easiest to fold is the direction of the grain. If there is resistance, or the paper cracks where it is folded then the grain is running in the opposite direction. All the grains should run parallel to the spine of a book.

Handmade papers generally have very little grain; this is because they are made in a frame or a deckle and mould, meaning that the fibres are laid down in a random fashion.

Rubber stamps

Rubber stamps are my tool of choice to decorate a book cover – they come in a huge range of styles, one to suit every taste! My personal taste ranges from the whimsical to the quirky through collage and distressed to elegant, old-fashioned and sometimes just weird!

You can buy stamps that are mounted on wood (my favourite), on clear acrylic, or unmounted. The choice is yours.

Ink pads

Ink pads are a very useful colouring medium. Used with rubber stamps, straightforward stamping gives you either a basic black image or a coloured image, depending on the ink pad. Ink pads can also be used to create backgrounds that can then be stamped over, create papers which can then be used to cover your books, and to edge card to give it definition. Stamped images can be coloured using paint, pens or crayons to give hundreds of variations from one stamp.

Dye ink pads

These are generally water-based and dry on contact with paper or card. There are many different makes of dye ink available in different colours and shades. Certain dye ink pads are slightly different in that they are designed to allow you to attain certain looks and finishes with them.

One range that falls into this category are distress ink pads, which are designed to stay wet longer than most dye inks. This allows you to use an embossing powder to give a raised, textured effect – or to spread the ink into an image stamped with it. In addition, these inks are not permanent, which means you can colour with them using a paintbrush and achieve lots of watercolour effects using them. I like to use distress ink pads a lot in my work as I love the effects that can be achieved with them.

If you want to watercolour over a stamped image you need to use a waterproof permanent archival ink so that it will not run. I use black for just about everything, but sepias and browns are great for certain effects.

Pigment inks

Like dye ink pads, these are water-based, but they have a thicker formulation and are generally more opaque than dye inks. Pigment inks can be used for a variety of techniques that can be used to decorate your book covers.

Most are also designed to be used with an embossing powder and so stay wet longer to allow the powder to be applied. Some pigment inks will never dry on their own without heat-setting or embossing. Others will dry by themselves fairly quickly, or they can be helped along with a heat gun.

Another types of ink pad that is available are Stazon inks. These are solvent based and used for particular types of project. Unlike water-based inks, these can be used on glass, metal and plastic.

Paint

I like to use acrylic paints to colour backgrounds which can then be stamped over, I also use them to paint images after stamping them.

You can buy a vast range of acrylic paints. My personal favourites are the Adirondack Dabber paints. These match the Adirondack range of ink pads, and so are great when used in combination.

Walnut ink stain

This product is walnut ink with added colours! They come with a dabber top for easy application and are another nice way to create a background that can be stamped over. Again, the finish is quite watery, which is the style I like.

Other colouring media

Another favourite thing I like to use to colour is watercolour pencil crayons. Applied with a brush or a waterbrush, these give a great effect and can be used as a background or to colour an image. I also use coloured marker pens and pencil crayons to colour images.

Binding and threads

Many, many things can be used to bind books. Here are just a few suggestions!

Threads Stranded embroidery thread, cotton thread, linen book-binding thread, macramé thread: all are suitable.

Ribbons Try lots of different widths, patterns and colours.

Wools and fibres These are normally used for knitting, crochet, embroidery and so forth, but they are very useful as bindings for books.

Wire Use thin wire instead of thread. It is a little more difficult to use, but much more fun!

Book rings These are metal rings that are hinged and open to allow them to be used to bind a book.

Bamboo skewers, **cocktail sticks** and **wooden coffee stirrers** Any of these would be fun to use for a piano-hinge book.

Elastic bands Use instead of thread to secure a piano-hinge binding.

Raffia Great fun for a garden-themed book.

String An everyday product that is a fun thing to use in a book project.

Embellishments

Eyelets Available in many different designs, shapes, sizes and colours. They can be used to reinforce and to decorate holes through which threads can be passed, or used purely as decorative features in their own right.

Brads These paper fasteners come in a multitude of colours, shapes, sizes and designs. They are great as decorative additions, and can be used to attach other decorative elements – especially those with holes already in them, such as charms. They can also be used to attach paper pieces together, wrap threads around or as part of a fastening or closure for a book.

Buttons These make fun decorative additions to a design and can be attached with or without thread added through the holes. They can also be added as part of a binding by passing the binding thread through them, or used as part of a fastening or closure for a book.

Metal charms Available in a huge range of designs to suit any theme, many have holes which allow you to attach them to your books with brads. Others can be glued in place.

Jewellery findings Jump rings of various sizes can be used to attach elements with holes, such as charms. They can also be used to join things together. Broken pieces of jewellery picked up in charity or junk shops make great additions to a piece.

Haberdashery Buckles, press studs, pins with fancy tops, lace, braids and sequins all make interesting additions to designs.

Sewing machine This can be used to sew pieces together to use as decorative elements, or you can hand-sew designs on to a piece and use the machine to join separate pieces together.

Paper embellishments Using paper punches and die-cutting systems, you can make your own to match the papers used in the rest of the design. Gold-coloured paper elements can be used as decorations, and stickers are also useful additions to designs.

Metal embellishments Metal borders can be used to edge covers and pages, and metal clips used to decorate page edges. Metal sheet, used in combination with punches, can make interesting embellishments. Paper clips of various colours, shapes and sizes are fun additions, and wire can be used to fasten things together and to make decorative elements.

Beads Dangle these from the ends of binding threads. They can be useful as part of the binding, adding them as you go along, or you can simply glue them on as decoration.

Found objects Bits and pieces that you have lying around can be utilised as part of a design. For example, some bottle tops have great designs on them. Washers, nuts and bolts give an industrial feel, while hinges from a DIY shop can be used as functional and decorative pieces.

Other materials and equipment

Craft knife Use either a disposable knife or one that has replacement blades to ensure you are using a sharp edge when you are cutting.

Cutting mat Use a self healing mat to protect your work surface.

Metal ruler Used for measuring and as a straight edge to cut against with a craft knife. Do not use a plastic ruler to cut against, as you can cut into it and end up with an uneven edge.

Bone folder This provides a smooth surface to use when folding and scoring paper.

PVA glue This is white glue that dries clear. It can also be watered down if necessary.

Eyelet setter This is essential to secure eyelets to your work.

Diamond glaze Clear-drying very strong dimensional adhesive, this is useful for attaching embellishments.

Glue stick A semi-dry glue that is useful for securing papers.

Double-sided tape Dry tape adhesive, this is used to secure card to card, or paper to paper.

Hole punch Used for punching holes in paper, an office punch is ideal.

Japanese screw punch Different-sized heads are available, which give different-sized holes. This can be used anywhere.

Craft hole punches These come in lots of shapes and sizes and are useful for decoration, as well as hole punching.

Piercing tool This is useful for making small holes.

Heat gun Used for melting embossing powder and drying inks, paints and so forth.

Scissors Small and large sizes are useful for different tasks and to suit personal preference.

Paper punches These come in a variety of designs and are great for decoration.

Craft scissors These scissors have decorative edges and are fun to use to trim pages or around images for decoration.

Spray bottle This is used for creating watercolour effects for backgrounds.

Scrap paper Used to protect work surfaces when gluing, painting, inking and so forth.

Bulldog clips These are used to hold pages together while punching holes, and also to clamp pieces while glue dries.

Embossing tool This metal-ended tool is used with a ruler to make creases to fold.

Waterbrush A paint brush with an in-built water reservoir.

Die-cutting machine You can use embossing folders with this to decorate entire sheets of card in a very short time, or to make your own paper embellishments.

Basic techniques

Covering a board with a decorative paper is a technique that you will use in many book-making projects so it is a good idea to master it.

Covering a board with lighter-weight paper

A lighter-weight paper is the easiest type with which to cover a board because the corners can be tucked in, folded over and glued without producing much extra bulk.

1. Cut your board to the size you want, then place it on the back of your paper and trim the paper to leave a 2cm (1in) border around it.

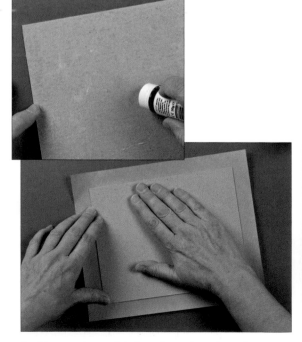

2. Use a glue stick (see inset) to attach the board to the middle of the paper.

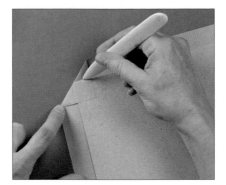

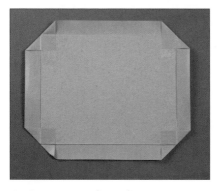

3. Apply a touch of glue to each corner of the board, fold over the paper, then use a bone folder to push the paper in as shown.

4. Repeat on the other corners, making sure to make a sharp crease on each.

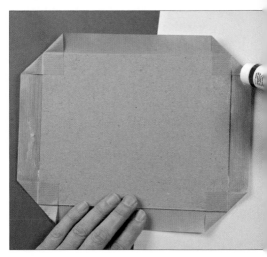

5. Put some scrap paper down and apply glue to the short edges of the paper.

Tip

When making creases, I prefer to turn the piece as I fold, and pull the paper towards me.

6. Pull the edges over, making sure that the paper is tight against the board, and sharpen the crease with a bone folder.

7. Repeat on the long sides.

8. Cut a piece of paper slightly smaller than the board, and glue it in place as an endpaper.

Covering a board with heavier-weight paper

A heavier-weight paper is a little more complicated to use as the corners need to be trimmed away, taking care not to trim too close as the corner can then poke through, before folding over and gluing. This gets rid of extra bulk and makes for a neater finish.

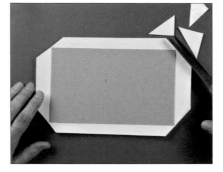

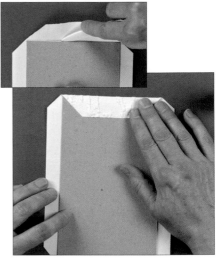

1. Cut your board to the size you want, then glue it to the back of your paper with a glue stick. Trim the paper to leave a 2cm (1in) border around the board.

2. Trim off all the corners with a pair of scissors. Do not trim them right up to the corner – leave a little paper as shown.

3. Run the bone folder down along the side of the board (see inset), then apply glue to the paper and fold it over.

5. Cut an end paper as before, and glue it in place.

4. Repeat on the opposite side, then use the point of the bone folder to tuck in the overlap on the corners (see inset). Crease, glue and fold the other sides as before.

Folding concertinas

This is another technique that you will use in many book-making projects.

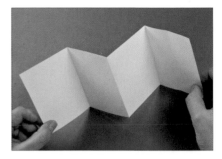

1. Fold your strip of card in half and sharpen the crease with the bone folder (see inset), then open it out.

2. Turn the piece over and fold each side into the centre. Crease the folds and open it out.

3. Close the concertina to finish, checking that it folds up correctly.

Note

When folding a concertina you create valley and mountain folds. These folds are so called as they resemble a range of mountains with valleys between them. A mountain fold is raised part of the paper and a valley fold is the one next to it that dips down.

Tip

An alternative method is to measure and score your strip of paper to give panels of a particular size.

My Heart Has Wings

Using a book ring is one of the simplest methods of binding a book: simply punch holes through the covers and pages and thread through a ring or number of rings. In addition to holding the book together, book rings give you a great place to add embellishments – either tied on or dangled from the rings.

For this book I have used three rings set into one side of the heart. This echoes the asymmetrical shape of the heart.

The template for this project can be found on page 78.

Note

The heart template is asymmetrical, so make sure that the decorative paper is glued to the front of the front cover and the back of the back cover.

You will need

- One A4 sheet of board
- One 30 x 30cm (12 x 12in) sheet of light-coloured bird-themed decorative paper
- One 30 x 30cm (12 x 12in) sheet of dark-coloured bird-themed decorative paper
- Ten A4 sheets of heavyweight white paper for pages
- One A4 sheet of green card
- One A4 sheet of thick card
- Straight scissors
- Glue stick
- Craft knife and cutting mat
- Japanese screw punch
- Heart eyelets and setting tool
- Scalloped-edge craft scissors
- Heart-shaped brads
- PVA glue
- Wing charms
- 20cm green ribbon
- Twig heart embellishment
- Scrap paper
- Sponge
- Green ink pad
- Small heart-shaped craft punch
- Double-sided sticky tape
- Spiral clip
- Three 25mm (1in) book rings
- Small charms

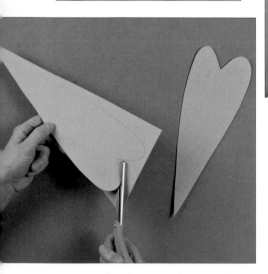

1. Transfer the template to the board and cut it out, then make a second copy. These will be the front and back covers.

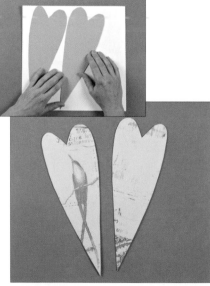

2. Use the glue stick to glue the light-coloured decorative paper to both covers (see inset), then use a craft knife and cutting mat to cut round each one.

3. Glue the dark-coloured decorative paper to the bare sides of the covers and cut them out.

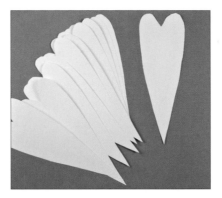

4. Cut out ten heart-shaped pages from the white paper, using the template to guide you.

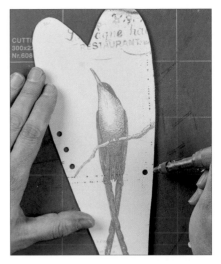

5. Place the front cover on the craft mat and use the Japanese screw punch to make three holes on the left and one on the right.

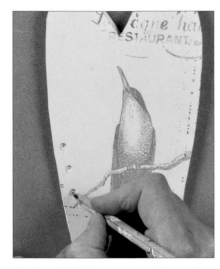

6. Stack the pages up, place the cover on top, and use a pencil to make marks in each of the holes on the left.

7. Remove the cover and punch through the stack of papers at each mark.

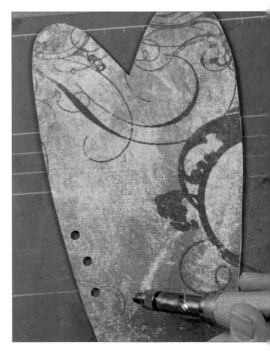

8. Place the front cover on the back cover (make sure that it is the right way round), mark the holes and punch them out.

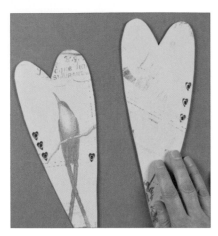

9. Use the eyelet-setting tool to secure four heart-shaped eyelets in the front cover. Repeat on the back cover, making sure the hearts face outwards.

10. Cut out a heart shape from the light-coloured paper offcuts using straight scissors, and a small rectangle using the scalloped-edge craft scissors. Mount the heart on green card and trim it to leave a small border. Mount both the heart and the rectangle on thick card.

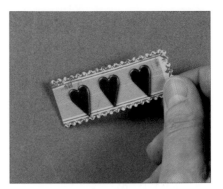

11. Punch three holes in the rectangle with the Japanese screw punch and secure a heart-shaped brad through each one.

12. Use PVA glue to attach two wing charms to the heart.

13. Wrap the ribbon around the twig heart, tying a knot to secure it at the end.

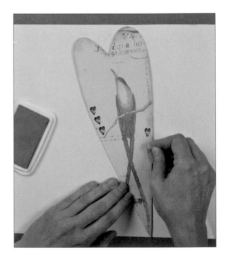

14. Put down some scrap paper. Use a sponge to apply green ink to the edge of the front cover with a brushing motion.

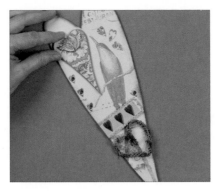

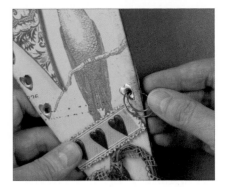

15. Use the heart punch to make three hearts from dark-coloured decorative paper offcuts and three from the light-coloured decorative paper offcuts. Use the glue stick to mount the light hearts on the dark hearts, then glue them to the front cover around the bird's head.

16. Use PVA glue to attach the twig heart at the bottom, and double-sided tape to attach the mounted paper embellishments.

17. Thread a spiral clip through the eyelet on the right-hand side.

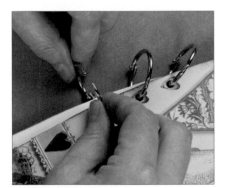

18. Hold the covers and pages in place and join them together with book rings.

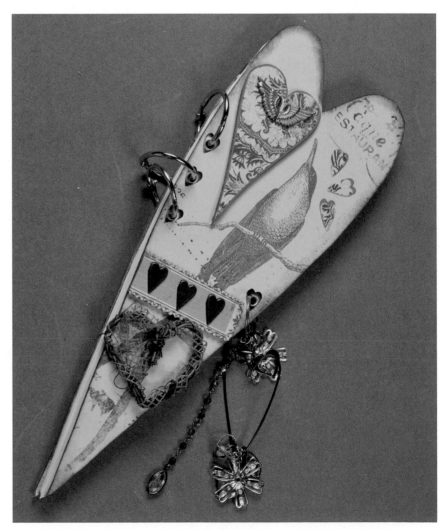

19. Attach the charms to the spiral clip to finish.

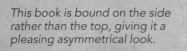
This book is bound on the side rather than the top, giving it a pleasing asymmetrical look.

Let's Face It...

One large ring is used here to fasten the covers and pages together. It also acts as a point from which to hang extra stamped embellishments.

In the Round

Several sizes of round pages are joined with one ring, which is then embellished by having ribbons and braids tied on to it.

Whimsey

This accordion book is simply a series of folded panels, so if you can fold a piece of card in half you can make it! The addition of decorative card to each panel gives the book extra strength and allows you to attach a ribbon, which is used to tie the book closed.

I like to use an echo of the image on the front and on the back of each panel; in this case just a small square of coloured card and a section of each image.

You will need

- One 60 x 18cm (23½ x 7in) sheet of white card
- Five 30.5 x 30.5cm (12 x 12in) sheets of decorative paper: one plain, two floral and two striped
- Six A5 sheets of thin white card
- 11.5 x 18cm (4½ x 7in) sheets of card: three green, six brown and three pink
- Glue stick
- Permanent black archival ink pad
- Stampington stamps: Clown Bebe (S7306), Top Hat Whimsey (S7302), Dramatic Jester (S7305), Star Juggler (S7300), Lovesick Moon (S7307)
- Waterbrush and fuchsia and yellow watercolour pencils
- 2mm (1 1/16in) hole punch
- Spiral clips
- Brads: heart, small flower and large flower
- Craft punches: large heart, small flower and large flower
- Craft knife and cutting mat
- Pencil, ruler and scissors
- 80cm (31½in) length of narrow ribbon
- 80cm (31½in) length of broad ribbon

1. Fold the 60 x 18cm (23½ x 7in) white card every 12cm (4¾in) to make a five panel accordion.

2. Cut five pieces of decorative paper to the same size as the five boards. Use a glue stick to attach one to each board to make decorative panels. Put the offcuts of decorative paper to one side.

3. Use a permanent ink pad with the Clown Bebe stamp to transfer the image to one of the A5 sheets of thin white card, then stamp again on an offcut of the plain decorative paper.

4. Cut out the hat, ruff and leggings from the image on decorative paper. Glue them in place on the image on thin white card, using a glue stick.

5. Draw a waterbrush across the tip of a fuchsia watercolour pencil (see inset), and use the colour to paint the arms, hat brim, belly and shaded part of the face of the image. Use the waterbrush with the yellow pencil to fill in the remaining areas. Note how the colours blend on the face.

6. Cut out the Clown Bebe image with a pair of scissors.

7. Glue him to a 5.5 x 12.5cm (2⅛ x 5in) piece of green card, then mount this on a 5.7 x 12.7cm (2¼ x 5⅛in) piece of brown card.

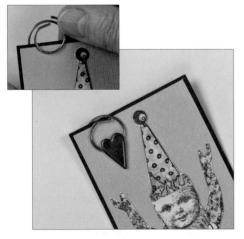

8. Slide a spiral clip on to the top (see inset), then punch a hole just inside the bottom of the spiral, using the hole punch. Secure a heart-shaped brad in the hole.

9. Glue the assembled piece on to one of the covered boards with a glue stick. Cut an 11.5 x 1cm (4½ x ⅝in) strip of green card from the offcuts, and glue it beneath the piece with the glue stick.

10. Use the large heart punch to punch a heart from the green card. Make a hole with the hole punch (see inset), then secure a heart-shaped brad in the hole before gluing it to the larger piece as shown. This completes the first inner panel.

11. Make another inside panel by stamping the Top Hat Whimsey twice on to thin white card and once on an offcut of the floral decorative paper. Cut out the skirt, bodice and head from the floral paper, and cut out the face from the thin white card before securing the parts in place on the remaining piece of white card. Cut out the figure and mount it on a 6.5 x 12cm (2½ x 4¾in) piece of pink card, then mount that on a 6.7 x 12.2cm (2⅝ x 4⅞in) piece of brown card. Mount this on a decorative panel, then glue a 18 x 0.5cm (7 x ¼in) strips of green card to the left and a 0.5 x 11.5cm (¼ x 4½in) strip below the figure. Make a heart as before (see step 10), using an offcut of the striped decorative paper instead of green; and punch three small flowers from offcuts of the plain decorative paper. Add a small flower brad to each, then attach all four of the paper embellishments as shown using the glue stick.

12. Stamp the Dramatic Jester once on white card and once on an offcut of the plain decorative paper. Cut out the hat and centre of the belly from the plain decorative paper, then secure the parts in place on the thin white card. Cut out the figure and mount it on a 6.5 x 11cm (2½ x 4in) piece of pink card, then mount that on a 6.7 x 11.2cm (2⅝ x 4⅛in) piece of brown card. Mount this on a decorative panel, then glue an 11.5 x 1cm (4½ x ½in) strip of pink card below the figure. Punch one large flower from the plain decorative paper offcuts and one from pink card, and secure them together with a large flower brad. Punch three small flowers from the plain decorative paper offcuts and add a small flower brad to each. Attach the four paper embellishments to the panel as shown using the glue stick.

13. Stamp the Star Juggler once on thin white card and once on an offcut of the striped decorative paper. Cut out the hat and clock face from the striped paper and glue the parts in place on the white piece. Cut out the figure and mount it on a 5.5 x 11cm (2⅛ x 4in) piece of pink card, then mount that on a 5.7 x 11.2cm (2¼ x 4½in) piece of brown card. Attach a spiral clip and large flower brad to the right-hand side and mount the piece on a decorative panel. Glue two 1 x 18cm (½ x 7in) strips of pink card to the right of the panel. Punch three large hearts from the offcuts of striped decorative paper and attach them to the panel using the glue stick.

14. Stamp the Lovesick Moon twice on white card and once on an offcut of the striped decorative paper. Cut out the body, legs, head and hat from the striped paper and glue the parts in place on the thin white card. Cut out the face from the second piece of white card and attach this on top. Cut out the figure and mount it on a 5.5 x 11cm (2⅛ x 4in) piece of green card, then mount that on a 5.7 x 11.2cm (2¼ x 4½in) piece of brown card. Attach a spiral clip to the left-hand side and mount the piece on a decorative panel. Punch a small flower from an offcut of the plain decorative paper, add a small flower brad to the centre and glue it in the figure's hands. Add a 11.5 x 1cm (4½ x ½in) strip of pink card below the figure and attach three heart brads, then add a 1 x 18cm (½ x 7in) strip of green card on the right. Punch three large hearts from an offcut of the plain decorative paper and three flowers from offcuts of the decorative striped paper. Glue the flowers on to the hearts, then glue large flower brads on top. Attach the assembled pieces on top of the green strip.

15. Make a detail by stamping the face of the Lovesick Moon on a 4cm (1½in) square of white card. Use the waterbrush to colour it with fuchsia and yellow watercolour pencils. When dry, mount it on a 4.2cm (1⅜in) square of brown card.

16. Mount a 6cm (2⅜in) square offcut of decorative floral paper on a 6.2cm (2½in) square of pink card. Mount this in the centre of an 11.5 x 18cm (4½ x 7in) panel of green card, then attach the mounted Lovesick Moon detail to complete the first outside panel.

17. Mount a decorative floral paper square offcut on green card and glue it on to a pink panel. Make a detail (see step 15) using the Star Juggler stamp; then mount the detail on the square, as shown.

18. Make a decorative floral paper square offcut and mount it on pink card. Glue it on to a green panel, then make a detail (see step 15) using the Dramatic Jester stamp. Mount the detail on the square, as shown.

19. Mount a square offcut of decorative floral paper on green card and glue it on to a pink panel. Make a detail (see step 15) using the Top Hat Whimsey stamp; then mount the detail on the square, as shown.

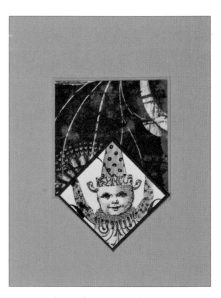

20. Make a final panel by gluing a square offcut of decorative floral paper on to a pink square and gluing it on to a green panel. Make a detail (see step 15) using the Clown Bebe stamp; then mount the detail on the square, as shown.

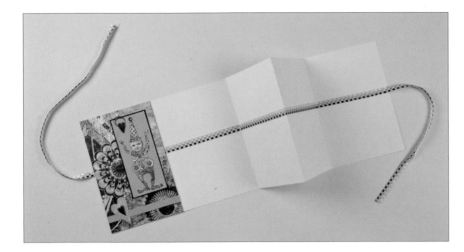

21. Use small squares of double-sided sticky tape to secure the narrow ribbon halfway up the inside, then use double-sided tape to attach the Clown Bebe panel as shown.

22. Attach the other inside panels with double-sided tape, making sure to leave a small gap by each hinge.

23. Turn the book over and attach a broad ribbon to the centre as before. Secure the outside panels, matching the stamps with the panels inside.

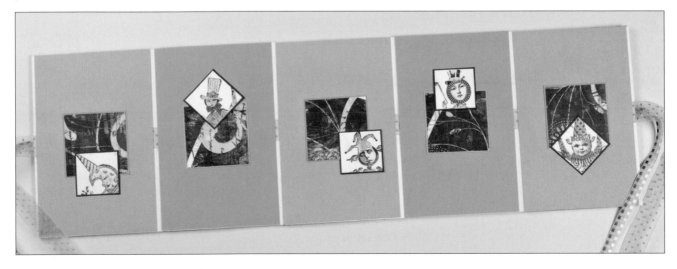

The completed book is a five-panel accordion-folded book decorated with preprinted papers and stamped images. It looks as beautiful closed as it does open!

She Sells Seashells

Lace, buttons and other haberdashery items are used to embellish this seaside-themed book.

Birds and Lanterns

Here, ribbon is used to link the panels of this accordion book and also to tie it closed.

Up My Street

Fun and funky houses with a garden fence and flowers at the back give a different look to this version of an accordion book.

Oriental Muse

I really like flag books. They look so spectacular and complicated when you open them and the pages (flags) move past each other; but in reality they are quite simple once you know the trick, which is just the placement of the flags on opposite sides of the accordion spine.

You will need

- Two 10 x 14cm (4 x 5½in) sheets of board
- Pad of red and mustard decorative paper 15 x 15cm (6 x 6in)
- Four pads of decorative paper 15 x 15cm (6 x 6in) in two sets of complementary designs
- A5 sheets of red, green, white and gold card
- One 20 x 10cm (8 x 4in) sheet of red card
- Card for flags: two 5 x 14cm (2 x 5½in), two 5 x 12cm (2 x 4¾in), two 5 x 10cm (2 x 4in) and two 5 x 8cm (2 x 3⅛in) pieces
- Glue stick and scissors
- Scalloped-edge craft scissors
- Craft knife and cutting mat
- Two adhesive metal edging strips
- Pencil and metal ruler
- Embossing stylus
- Double-sided sticky tape
- Stampington stamp: Puccini's Muse (P2201)
- Permanent black archival ink pad
- Green and red watercolour crayons and waterbrush
- Golden butterfly embellishment

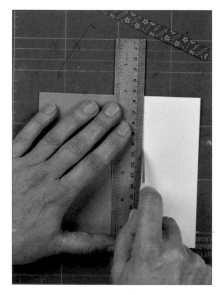

1. Use a glue stick to attach a piece of decorative red paper to one of the boards. Trim away the excess with a craft knife.

2. Cover the other side with green card, then repeat with the other board.

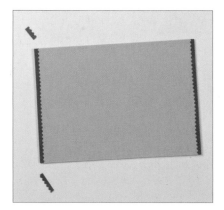

3. Use the scalloped-edge craft scissors to cut two narrow strips of red card. Stick one to each of the short edges on the green side of one of the boards, and trim to fit. This will be the back cover.

4. Attach an adhesive metal edging strip to the red side of the other board. This will be the front cover.

5. Use a pencil to make marks every 2cm (⅞in) on the long edges of the 20 x 10cm (8 x 4in) piece of red card. Use an embossing stylus and metal ruler to score lines between the pairs of marks, then fold the piece up into an accordion (see inset).

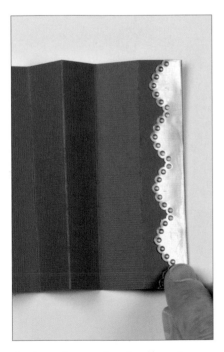

6. Attach an adhesive metal edging strip to one end.

7. Turn the piece over and cut a 2cm- (⅞in) wide strip of green card. Use the scalloped-edge scissors to make a decorative edge, and use double-sided tape to attach a piece to each end. Trim away any excess.

8. Turn the accordion over. Cut long thin scalloped strips from green card and attach pieces to either side of each valley fold as shown, using the glue stick. Trim away any excess.

9. Cover the longest and shortest pairs of flags with matching decorative papers, as shown. Note that each flag should have contrasting papers on opposite sides.

10. Cut a 1.5cm (½in) strip of green card. Fold it in half lengthways and trim it with the scalloped-edge scissors. Put some glue on the inside, then attach it to the end of one of the flags.

11. Trim the excess, then repeat on the other flags.

12. Decorate the other pairs of flags in the same way, using a different matching set of decorative papers.

13. Use double-sided tape to attach the covers to the inside of the accordion as shown, then attach a narrow scalloped-edged red strip to the inside of the front cover.

Note

Make sure the decorative metal edge of the accordion is attached to the outside of the front cover, as shown.

14. Using double-sided tape, attach one of the 14cm (5½in) flags to the lower right of the right-most mountain fold.

15. Secure the other 14cm (5½in) flag to the opposite side of the same mountain fold. The flags should point in opposite directions and have the contrasting papers showing. Ensure you leave a gap between the flags so that they can move freely past each other as you close the book.

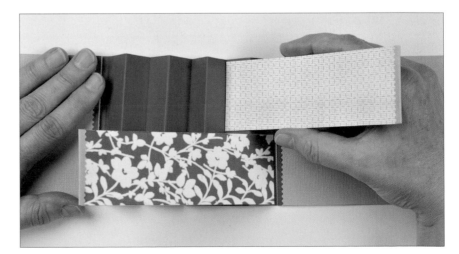

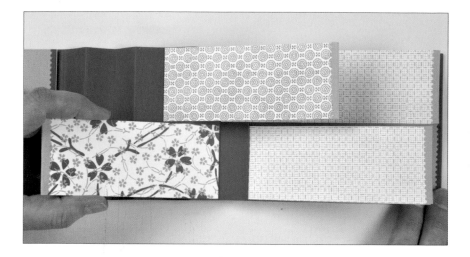

16. Fold the flags down to the right and attach the 12cm (4¾in) flags to the next mountain fold to the left. Again, ensure the flags line up and do not block any of the others when the book opens and closes.

17. Attach the 10cm (4in) and 8cm (3⅛in) flags in the same way, then close the book and put it to one side.

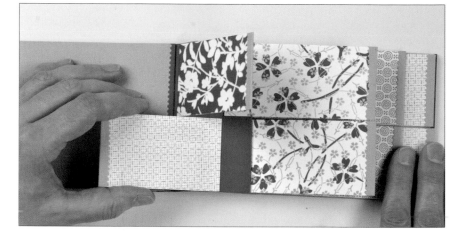

18. Ink the Puccini's Muse stamp with permanent black and stamp it on to a 5.7 x 8.7cm (2½ x 3⅜in) piece of white card.

19. Brush the ink pad across the edges of the card to give a faded border.

20. Use the waterbrush with the green and red watercolour pencils to decorate the image.

21. Mount the image on a 6 x 9cm (2⅛ x 3½in) piece of red card with double-sided tape, then mount that on top of a 6.2 x 9.2cm (2½ x 3⅜in) piece of gold card.

22. Brush the golden butterfly embellishement with the ink pad (see inset), then attach the mounted image on the front cover using double-sided tape. Finish the book by attaching the butterfly to the cover with a little double-sided tape.

The completed book.

The beauty of a flag book is the effect when opened, but a striking cover will make all the difference when it is closed.

*This is the inside of the Oriental Muse book,
showing how the flags move past each other.*

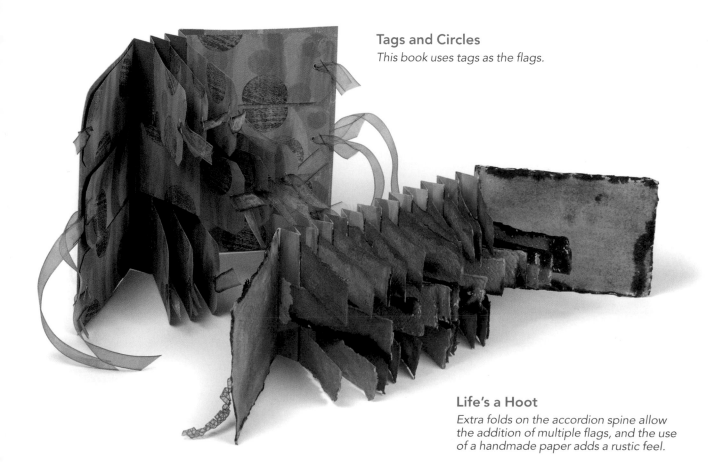

Tags and Circles
This book uses tags as the flags.

Life's a Hoot
*Extra folds on the accordion spine allow
the addition of multiple flags, and the use
of a handmade paper adds a rustic feel.*

Oh My Goth!

This book introduces stitching as a way of binding a book together. If you have never made a stitched book before, this is a good place to start.

Simply use the binding guide to punch or pierce five holes through the fold of the cover and pages, then stitch them together with embroidery thread.

The binding guide template for the Oh My Goth! project, shown at full size.

1 ○

2 ○

3 ○

4 ○

5 ○

You will need

- 30 x 20cm (11⅞ x 7⅞in) sheets of handmade paper in lilac, orange and purple
- Three 32 x 26cm (12½ x 10¼in) sheets of white handmade paper
- A4 sheets of purple and lilac paper
- A5 sheets of card in pale pink, orange and black
- Straight scissors
- Glue stick
- Scrap of cardboard for binding guide
- 2mm (1¹⁄₁₆in) hole punch
- Pencil and ruler
- Cutting mat and piercing tool
- Large-eyed needle
- Purple and orange embroidery thread
- Small wire brush
- Permanent black archival ink pad
- Orange ink pad
- Stampotique stamp: Spykee (6023R)
- Fine-nibbed pink felt tip pen
- Waterbrush
- Double-sided sticky tape

1. Cut the two pieces of handmade paper to 30 x 20cm (11⅞ x 7⅞in). Put the lilac one on top of the purple. Fold both in half, then open them out. This will be the cover of the book.

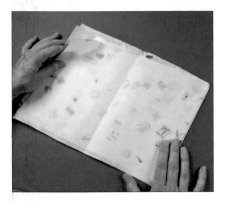

2. Repeat this with three pieces of handmade paper, each cut to be 32 x 26cm (12½ x 10¼in). These will be the pages.

3. Cut a 30 x 8cm (11⅞ x 3⅛in) strip of purple paper. Fold it in half, then cut it to a point at the open end. Open it up.

4. Cut a 30 x 8cm (11⅞ x 3⅛in) strip of lilac paper, fold it in half, then trim the open end to an angle. Open it up.

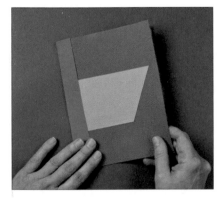

5. Use a glue stick to attach the lilac strip to the purple outer cover, folding it round. Next, glue a 6cm- (2⅜in) wide strip of orange paper to the spine, folding it round and trimming any excess.

6. Wrap the purple strip around the lilac inner cover, then put it inside the purple outer cover.

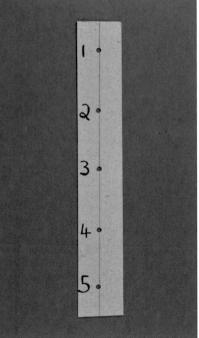

7. Transfer the binding guide template to cardboard, then use a hole punch to make the holes.

8. Open the cover out, place the pages inside, and use a pencil with the binding guide to mark five dots on the fold of the inside pages, as shown.

Tip

The inside pages are larger than the cover, so fold the pages up to ensure that the bottom of the binding guide is lined up with the bottom of the cover.

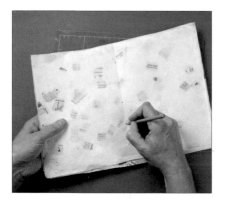

9. Place the opened book on a cutting mat and use a piercing tool to pierce the marked holes.

10. Thread a large-eyed needle with 1m (39in) of both orange and purple thread.

11. Turn the book over and take the needle down through hole 3, leaving a tail of at least 20cm (7⅞in).

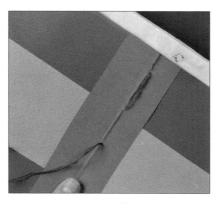

12. Bring the needle and thread up through hole 2, then down through hole 1.

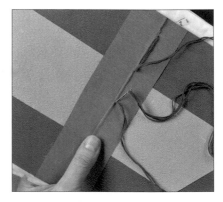

13. Bring the thread up through hole 2, then down hole 3.

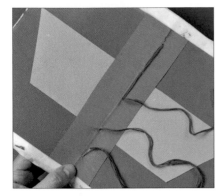

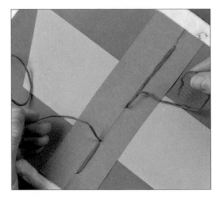

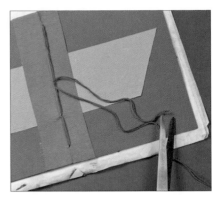

14. Bring the thread up through hole 4, then down hole 5.

15. Bring the thread back up through hole 4, then take the tail in one hand and the thread from hole 4 in the other.

16. Tie a knot, making sure it sits on hole 3 once tightened. Trim the ends of the thread to 18cm (7in) or so.

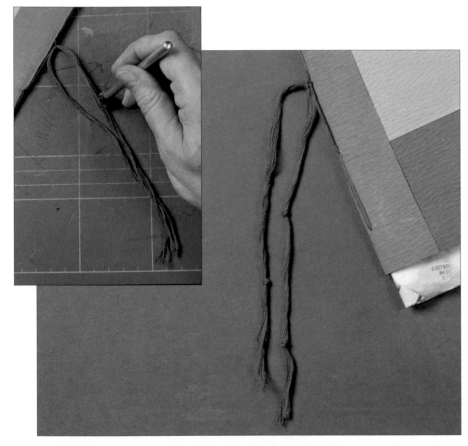

17. Draw a small wire brush down the thread ends repeatedly, to separate the threads (see inset), then tie two overhand knots in each by making a loop and drawing the end through.

18. Put the book to one side and use permanent black ink to stamp the Spykee stamp on to a 5.5 x 13cm (2⅛ x 5⅛in) piece of pale pink card.

20. Press the orange ink pad on to a plastic plate or other non-absorbant surface, then pick up the ink with the waterbrush and paint loosely round the figure.

19. Use a fine-nibbed pink felt tip pen to colour in details and add some extra hair to the figure.

21. Use double-sided sticky tape to mount the picture on black card, then on to orange, then black and finally pink, trimming each down to leave a 2mm border round the previous layer.

22. Use a glue stick to attach scraps and offcuts of the lilac, purple and orange handmade papers to the front cover, then attach the picture with double-sided sticky tape.

The completed book.

Beaded Flowers

An accordion-folded book with sets of pages sewn into the folds. Beads were added to the threads used to stitch the pages in place.

Bird Cage

A tag-shaped book where the pages are sewn on to the flat edge of the folded over spine.

Teatime

Handmade paper was used here to make pages of different sizes.

Stalks

In this small book, the back cover is longer than the front and folds over to be tucked into a slit cut into the front cover.

Opposite:

A very distinctive and striking book, this would be perfect as a gift – if you can bear to give it away!

Road Trip

Stab stitching is a traditional form of book binding in which the covers are attached to the pages using decorative stitching. Features of stab binding are that the thread, ribbon or cord used for the stitching should pass around the outside edge of the covers and that each hole is sewn through several times.

In this project I have used a very simple stitching pattern which is a good place to start before moving on to more complicated patterns.

The binding guide template for the Road Trip project, shown at full size.

1 ○

2 ○

3 ○

You will need

- Twelve 30 x 21cm (11⅞ x 8¼in) pieces of brown wrapping paper
- Two 21 x 15cm (8¼ x 6in) sheets of board
- A5 sheets of dark cream, brown and green card
- Yellow, green and brown permanent ink pads
- Craft knife, metal ruler and cutting mat
- Scrap paper
- Straight scissors
- Glue stick
- Bulldog clip
- Scrap of cardboard for binding guide
- 2mm (1¹/₁₆in) hole punch
- Pencil
- Japanese screw punch
- Large-eyed needle
- 150cm (59in) ribbon
- Stampington stamp: The Car (K5521)
- Three square brads
- Double-sided sticky tape
- Diamond glaze clear-drying glue
- Small compass charm

1. Crumple up a 30 x 21cm (11⅞ x 8¼in) piece of brown wrapping paper and unfurl it.

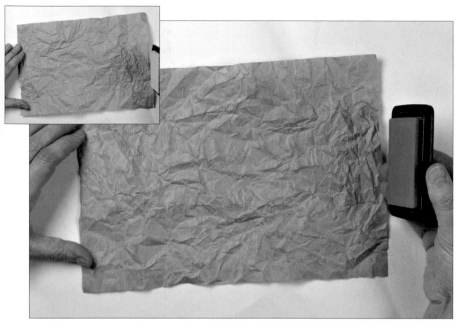

3. Crumple the paper up again and unfurl it. Repeat the brushing, this time using the brown ink pad.

2. Flatten it out on top of some scrap paper and gently brush the yellow ink pad over the whole piece (see inset). Do the same with the green ink pad.

4. Trim a 3cm (1⅛in) piece off the end of one of the boards.

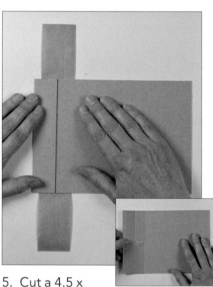

5. Cut a 4.5 x 30cm (1¾ x 11⅞in) strip of brown wrapping paper and glue the pieces of board to it with a glue stick, making sure to leave a small gap between them. Fold the rest of the strip round and glue it in place as a reinforcing strip (see inset).

6. Turn the inked paper face down and glue the board in the centre.

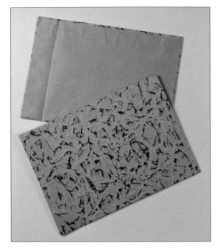

7. Cover the board as shown on pages 14–15, adding an endpaper of plain brown wrapping paper. Make a second board from a 21 x 15cm (8¼ x 6in) piece, and cover as for the first. These will be the book covers.

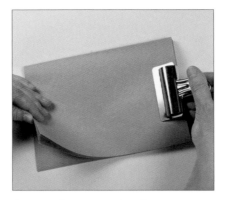

8. Cut the remaining brown paper into 21 x 15cm (8¼ x 6in) pieces. Use a bulldog clip to hold them straight and together. These will be the pages.

9. Make a binding guide by transferring the template to cardboard and punching the holes with a hole punch.

10. Use the binding guide with a pencil to mark the insides of both covers and the papers.

11. Use the Japanese screw punch to punch holes through the marks.

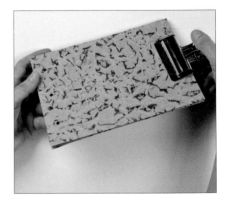

12. Put the pages between the covers, align the holes and hold everything in place with a bulldog clip.

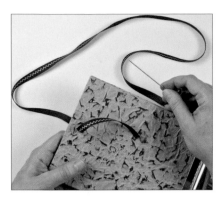

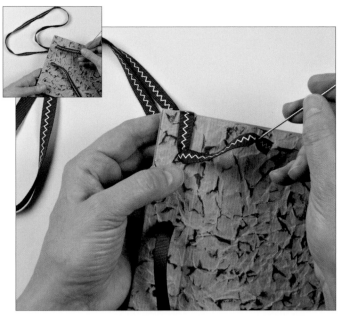

13. Thread the ribbon on to a large-eyed needle and take it down through hole 2, leaving a 8cm (3⅛in) tail.

Tip

If you are using a patterned ribbon, make sure it lies flat with the pattern showing at each stage of your work.

14. Bring the needle up through hole 1 (see inset), then take it over the top and back up through hole 1.

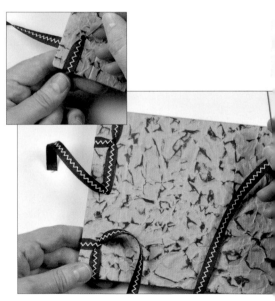

15. Pull the ribbon through, then take it round the spine and back up through hole 1 once more.

16. Take the needle down through hole 2 and up through hole 3.

17. Pull the ribbon through, take it round the bottom of the book and up through hole 3 (see inset). Next, take it round the spine and back up through hole 3 once more.

18. Remove the needle and take the remaining ribbon under and round the tail to start a knot on top of hole 2.

19. Take the ribbon over and round itself to finish the knot. Trim it to shape as shown using a pair of scissors, then remove the bulldog clip.

20. Cut a piece of dark cream card down to 7.5 x 8cm (3 x 3⅛in), then use permanent brown ink to stamp the car on to it.

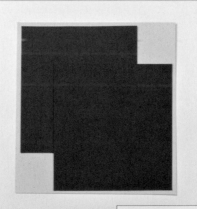

21. Use double-sided sticky tape to mount the stamped image on to brown card, then green card, trimming each in turn to leave a narrow border, as shown.

22. Mount two 7 x 7.5cm (2¾ x 3in) pieces of brown card on a 9.5 x 10cm (3¾ x 4in) piece of cream card. Attach the brown pieces as shown using double-sided sticky tape, then attach the mounted image in the centre (see inset).

23. Cut away the excess cream card using a craft knife, metal ruler and cutting mat.

24. Remove the arms from the brads and use diamond glaze adhesive to glue them in place on the front of the piece.

25. Use double-sided sticky tape to secure the piece in the centre of the front cover.

26. Tie a knot in a 5cm (2in) length of ribbon and use diamond glaze to secure it in the corner of the piece. Glue a small compass charm below the knot.

The completed book.

Sturdy but attractive, this type of book is perfect for taking notes while travelling – or just to perch on your shelf!

Clockwise from top left:

Initial

Blown vinyl wallpaper coloured with watercolour crayons was used to cover this book. A metalwork initial 'S' finishes it off. The binding guide template can be found on page 79.

Red Door

A house-shaped book with the stab stitched binding to one side. The fun paper used to cover the book was a sheet of wrapping paper. This book uses the same binding guide template as the Road Trip project.

Birds in a Tree

A simple stamped image and a metal charm add to the overall elegant look of this book. The binding guide template can be found on page 79.

African Lilies

This method of binding produces piano hinge books. Rest assured that it looks a lot more complicated than it actually is!

I have used wooden kebab skewers for this book, but you could also lots of other things, such as coffee stirrers, cocktail sticks, chopsticks, thin pencils, knitting needles or crochet hooks, to suit the theme of your book.

You will need

- Two 21 x 15cm (8¼ x 6in) sheets of purple card
- Eight 21 x 15cm (8¼ x 6in) sheets of pale pink paper
- Eight 21 x 15cm (8¼ x 6in) sheets of lilac paper
- Small piece of cardboard for binding guide
- Pencil
- Straight scissors
- Seven bamboo skewers
- Cranberry paint dabber
- 100cm (39in) black wool
- Double-sided sticky tape
- A5 sheet of white satin card
- A5 sheet of black card
- Purple, brown and red ink pads
- Spray bottle
- Permanent black archival ink pad
- Stampendous stamps: Agapanthus cluster (P107)
- Scrap paper

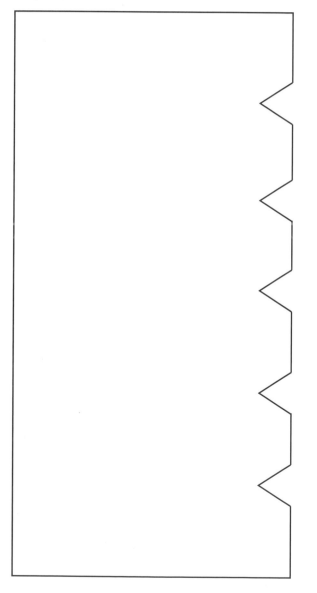

The template for the African Lilies project, shown at full size.

1. Take a 21 x 15cm (8¼ x 6in) piece of purple card and fold it in half. Transfer the template to cardboard and place it on the fold as shown. Mark the notches with a pencil.

2. Cut out all the notches with scissors, then make a second piece in the same way. These will be the covers of the book.

3. Stack four 21 x 15cm (8¼ x 6in) pieces of pink paper and fold them all in half. Mark the notches on the fold using the template and pencil, then cut them out as before.

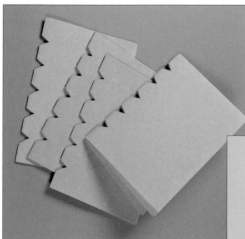

4. Do the same with another stack of four pieces of pink paper; and two stacks of four pieces of lilac paper to make all the pages for the book.

5. Paint the seven bamboo skewers with cranberry paint and allow them to dry thoroughly.

6. Take the front cover and first set of pink pages and hold them part-open as shown.

7. Slide a skewer inside the cover, taking it through the first notch and the pink pages to the second notch.

8. Slide the skewer through and under the cover to the third notch.

10. Place the first set of lilac pages against the pink, then slide another skewer through, using the tabs of the pink pages' spine that were not used with the first skewer.

9. Continue sliding the skewer through, alternating at each notch, until it holds the cover and pages together. This will leave some tabs unused. These will be used to secure the other pages.

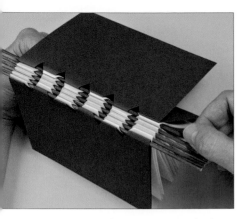

11. Repeat the process with the second set of lilac pages, then the second set of pink pages, and finally the back cover.

12. Slide the remaining skewers through the unused tabs of the front and back covers.

13. Find the middle of a 100cm (39in) length of wool and loop it over the rearmost skewer. Tie a simple knot.

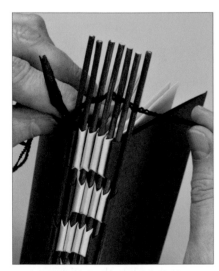

14. Take one end of the wool and weave it under and over the skewers.

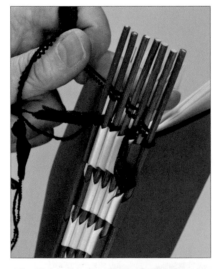

15. Take it round the frontmost skewer, and then weave it back to the rearmost skewer.

16. Continue weaving it back and forth until you have made a 2cm (¾in) border. Secure it with a knot made using both ends of the wool, then trim. Repeat on the bottom of the skewers. As well as being decorative, the weaving keeps the skewers in place.

17. Run double-sided tape down the insides of the front cover as shown, and close it to stiffen it and make the cover neater. Do the same to the back cover, then put the book to one side.

18. Take a 7 x 13.5cm (2¾ x 5⅜in) piece of white satin card and place it on scrap paper to protect your surface. Touch the non-permanent ink pads over the card to create a pattern.

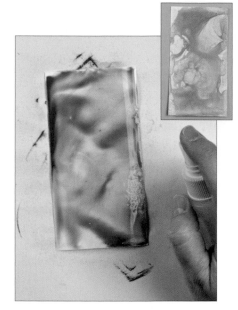

19. While the ink is still wet, use the spray bottle to mist the card with clean water. This causes the colours to mix and blend. Allow the card to dry (see inset).

20. Use the permanent black ink pad to stamp the main image in the centre of the panel, then stamp a few more times in a loose fashion around it to add some variation to the design.

21. Mount the panel on a piece of black card using double-sided tape. Cut the black card down to leave a narrow border round the white card, then mount the panel on the front cover with double-sided tape.

22. Make another panel and cut it down to 2.5 x 8.5cm (1 x 3⅜in). Mount it on a piece of black card and secure it on the lower left of the back cover.

The completed book.

Once bound into the spine, this technique makes for a distinctive, handsome and striking type of book.

Clockwise from top left:

Girl With a Ruler
This book uses rubber bands in place of wool to hold the skewers in place.

Anyone for Cappuccino?
The hinge of this book is made from coffee stirrers.

Swirl
This little book uses cocktail sticks, showing that even tiny books can look beautiful with this technique.

Autumn Leaves

This is the most complex and eye-catching project in this book, and probably the most rewarding. When you open it and fold the covers back to back, a star shape is revealed, and is sure to impress.

Accurate measuring of the pages and on the stitching is the secret to success. The stitching may seem a little fiddly at first, but it is quite straightforward once you get into the rhythm of it.

The multiple pages also leave lots of space for decorating. Having said that, the embossed texture of the paper I used here needs very little extra decoration, just a fun spider in the middle!

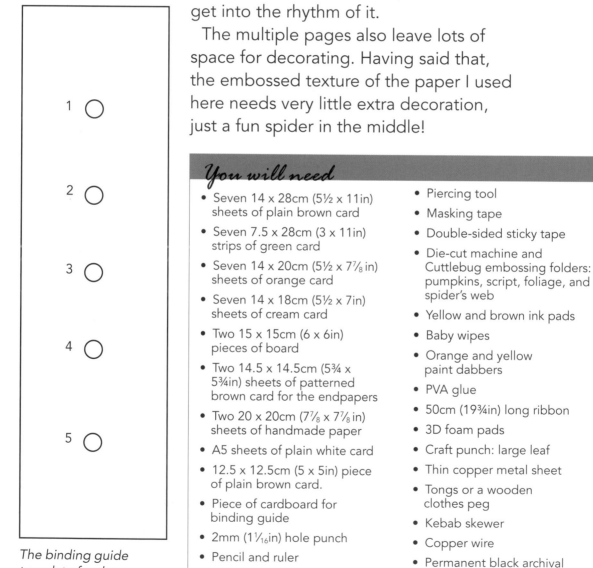

1 ○

2 ○

3 ○

4 ○

5 ○

The binding guide template for the Autumn Leaves project, shown at full size.

You will need

- Seven 14 x 28cm (5½ x 11in) sheets of plain brown card
- Seven 7.5 x 28cm (3 x 11in) strips of green card
- Seven 14 x 20cm (5½ x 7⅞ in) sheets of orange card
- Seven 14 x 18cm (5½ x 7in) sheets of cream card
- Two 15 x 15cm (6 x 6in) pieces of board
- Two 14.5 x 14.5cm (5¾ x 5¾in) sheets of patterned brown card for the endpapers
- Two 20 x 20cm (7⅞ x 7⅞ in) sheets of handmade paper
- A5 sheets of plain white card
- 12.5 x 12.5cm (5 x 5in) piece of plain brown card.
- Piece of cardboard for binding guide
- 2mm (1¹⁄₁₆in) hole punch
- Pencil and ruler
- 200cm (78¾in) brown stranded embroidery thread
- Needle
- Piercing tool
- Masking tape
- Double-sided sticky tape
- Die-cut machine and Cuttlebug embossing folders: pumpkins, script, foliage, and spider's web
- Yellow and brown ink pads
- Baby wipes
- Orange and yellow paint dabbers
- PVA glue
- 50cm (19¾in) long ribbon
- 3D foam pads
- Craft punch: large leaf
- Thin copper metal sheet
- Tongs or a wooden clothes peg
- Kebab skewer
- Copper wire
- Permanent black archival ink pad
- Craft stamp: Stampotique's Mr Stripes (6007H)

1. Fold one of the plain brown pieces of card in half.

2. Fold one of the green strips in half vertically, then horizontally to make an inner hinge.

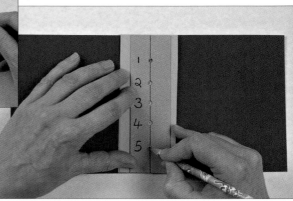

3. Transfer the template to cardboard to make a binding guide and punch the holes with the hole punch. Put the strip of green card on the spine of the brown card, with the fold on top. Place the binding guide on top and use a pencil to mark each hole.

4. Use a piercing tool to make the holes and complete one of the inner pages. Make six more inner pages in the same way.

5. Thread your needle with 200cm (78¾in) of brown thread and draw it up through hole 1 of the first inner page. Use a small piece of masking tape to secure the thread.

6. Hold the second inner page against the first inner page as shown, making sure the folds of the green inner hinges are matching.

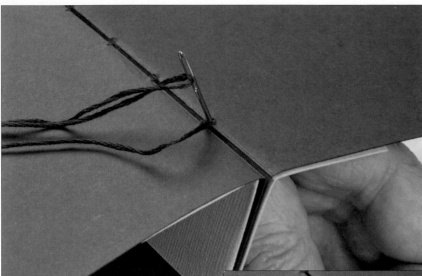

7. Take the needle down into hole 1 of the second inner page.

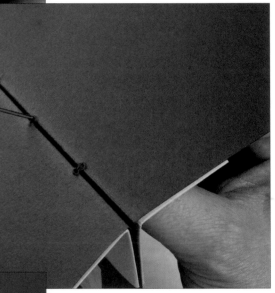

8. Pull the thread through, then take it up through hole 2 of the second inner page.

9. Pull the thread through, then take it down through hole 2 of the first inner page and up through hole 3 of the first inner page.

10. Take it down hole 3 of the second inner page and up through hole 4 of the second inner page, then down hole 4 of the first inner page and up hole 5 of the first inner page.

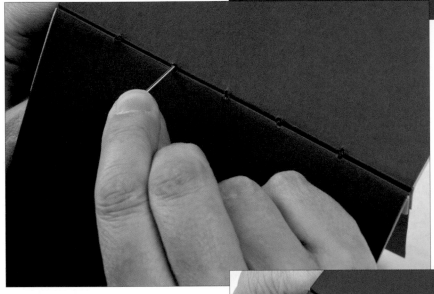

11. Take the needle down hole 5 of the second inner page, then up through hole 4 of the second inner page.

12. Take the needle down through hole 4 of the first set of inner pages and up through hole 3 of the first set.

13. Continue working in this 'down, up and across' fashion until the needle is at hole 1 of the first set of inner pages.

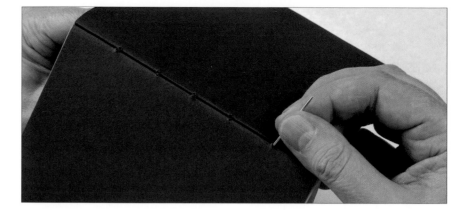

14. Pull the thread through, then take the needle between the inner pages and behind the threads at hole 1, as shown.

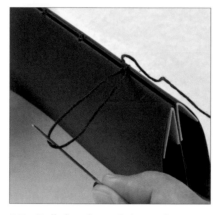

15. Pull the thread through to make a loop, then take the needle through the loop to make a knot.

16. Pull the knot tight, then hold the third inner page next to the second. Take the needle down hole 1 of the third inner page.

17. Follow the sequence outlined in steps 7–16 to secure the third inner page to the second.

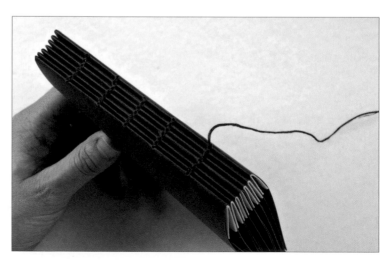

18. Add the other inner pages in the same way, remembering to check the green hinges are the correct way up each time.

19. Having made the last knot, take the needle back down hole 1 of the last inner page and under the loop between holes 1 and 2.

20. Make a loop and pass the needle through two or three times to secure the loose thread. Trim the excess, then remove the anchoring masking tape in the first inner page and do the same with the tail of the thread.

21. Run double-sided tape between the inner pages (see inset), then press them together to finish the basic book.

22. Fold an orange piece of card in half and use double-sided tape to attach one of the ends to the edge of the first inner page (see inset). Tape the other end to the edge of the opposite page. Note how the spine does not reach the spine of the inner page.

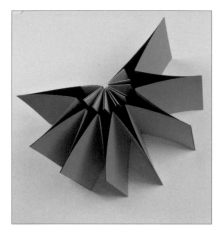

23. Tape folded orange card into each of the remaining inner pages.

24. Fold one of the pieces of cream card in half and put it in the pumpkin embossing folder.

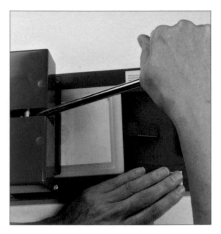

25. Use the die-cut machine to emboss the design on the card.

26. Open the card up and place it on scrap paper. Lightly brush the yellow ink pad across the surface of the card.

27. Repeat with the brown ink pad, brushing it lightly across the surface, allowing some yellow to show through.

28. Blend the colours together by rubbing a baby wipe lightly across the surface.

Note

Do not rub too hard as you can lift the surface off if the card gets too wet.

29. Add some orange and yellow dabs of paint to the card.

30. Blend the paint in using a baby wipe.

31. Brush the brown ink pad over the surface again, to reinforce and strengthen the colour.

32. Make six more card panels: two with the script folder, two with the foliage folder, one more with the pumpkin folder and one with the spider's web folder. Do not add paints to the spider's web card panel.

33. Secure these panels to the inner pages in the same way as the orange pieces. Make sure that they are the right way up and that the spider's web panel is in the middle of the book.

34. Use PVA glue to cover the two boards with handmade paper, as shown on pages 14–15, using patterned brown card for the endpapers.

35. Attach the ribbon to the book using double-sided tape, running it down the middle (see inset). Attach the covers, again using double-sided tape.

36. Make four 6 x 6cm (2$\frac{3}{8}$ x 2$\frac{3}{8}$in) squares of white card and decorate them in the same way as the pages. Use double-sided tape to attach them as shown to a 12.5 x 12.5cm (5 x 5in) piece of brown card.

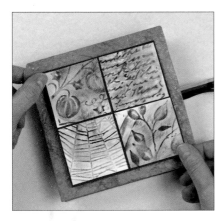

37. Attach the panel to the front of the book using 3D foam pads.

38. Use the large leaf punch to punch three leaves from thin copper sheet.

39. Hold each leaf over the gas flame of your hob (or a candle) until the metal acquires a patina. Be careful, and use tongs or a wooden clothes peg to hold them.

Tip
You can stop the colour change of the leaf at any time by dipping it into cold water.

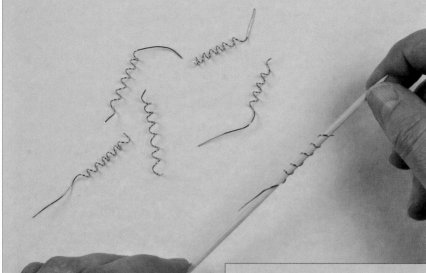

40. Wind a 10cm (4in) piece of wire round a kebab skewer, then slide it off. Make five more in the same way.

41. Wrap two coils round each leaf and bend the ends round the back. Secure them with foam pads as shown.

42. Stamp the Mr Stripes stamp on to white card, using permanent black ink. Colour the spider in with the yellow and orange paints (see inset), then cut it out and attach it to the spider's web page using double-sided tape.

The completed book.

Use the ribbons to tie the book open in the distinctive star shape.

A carefully completed star book is eye-catching and beautiful, whether fully open, partially open or even closed. The embossed texture of the pages used here means that they need very little extra decoration.

In the Woods
A slightly simpler version of a star book, this has windows cut into the pages to reveal more images underneath.

Haberdashery
Lots and lots of bits of fabric, ribbon, braid, buttons and other embellishments were used to decorate this star book.

Templates

These templates are shown at full size, except where noted.

The binding guide template for the My Heart Has Wings project (see page 18), shown at three quarters of the actual size. You will need to enlarge it to 133 per cent on a photocopier.

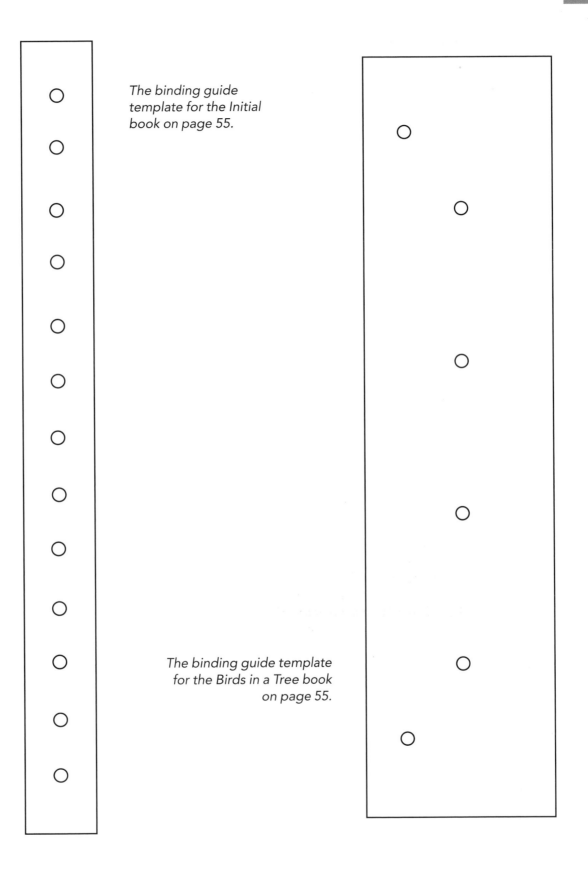

The binding guide template for the Initial book on page 55.

The binding guide template for the Birds in a Tree book on page 55.

Index

Book rings were used to bind this alphabet-themed piece. It would be perfect to use as an address book.